This plann

MW00484041

Name:

Phone:

Email:

Emergency Phone Numbers

Police:

Fire Station:

Poison Control:

Doctor:

Pediatrician:

Dentist:

Service Garage:

Towing:

School Phone Numbers

Amy Knapp

sourcebooks

Jewish and Muslim holidays begin at sundown.

Published by Sourcebooks
P.O. Box 4410, Naperville, Illinois 60567-4410
(630) 961-3900
sourcebooks.com

Printed and bound in China.
OGP 10 9 8 7 6 5 4 3 2 1

How to use *Amy Knapp's* Family Organizer

Weekly inspirational quotes

Create a weekly menu based on activities & appointments for the week

A comprehensive grocery list saves time & money at the store

Weekly list helps define & track important tasks

Current and following month-at-a-view calendars

Color-coded stickers mark events & appointments for quick reference

Week-at-a-view calendar

Mom's Goals

What's been working

What could be better

New goals to focus on

Self-care ideas

What I'm grateful for

Family Goals

What's been working

What we could do better

New goals to focus on

Adventures to have together

Volunteer ideas

2023

JANUARY

S	M	T	W	T	F	S
1	2	3	4	5	6	7
8	9	10	11	12	13	14
15	16	17	18	19	20	21
22	23	24	25	26	27	28
29	30	31				

FEBRUARY

S	M	T	W	T	F	S
			1	2	3	4
5	6	7	8	9	10	11
12	13	14	15	16	17	18
19	20	21	22	23	24	25
26	27	28				

MARCH

S	M	T	W	T	F	S
			1	2	3	4
5	6	7	8	9	10	11
12	13	14	15	16	17	18
19	20	21	22	23	24	25
26	27	28	29	30	31	

APRIL

S	M	T	W	T	F	S
						1
2	3	4	5	6	7	8
9	10	11	12	13	14	15
16	17	18	19	20	21	22
23	24	25	26	27	28	29
30						

MAY

S	M	T	W	T	F	S
	1	2	3	4	5	6
7	8	9	10	11	12	13
14	15	16	17	18	19	20
21	22	23	24	25	26	27
28	29	30	31			

JUNE

S	M	T	W	T	F	S
				1	2	3
4	5	6	7	8	9	10
11	12	13	14	15	16	17
18	19	20	21	22	23	24
25	26	27	28	29	30	

JULY

S	M	T	W	T	F	S
						1
2	3	4	5	6	7	8
9	10	11	12	13	14	15
16	17	18	19	20	21	22
23	24	25	26	27	28	29
30	31					

AUGUST

S	M	T	W	T	F	S
		1	2	3	4	5
6	7	8	9	10	11	12
13	14	15	16	17	18	19
20	21	22	23	24	25	26
27	28	29	30	31		

SEPTEMBER

S	M	T	W	T	F	S
					1	2
3	4	5	6	7	8	9
10	11	12	13	14	15	16
17	18	19	20	21	22	23
24	25	26	27	28	29	30

OCTOBER

S	M	T	W	T	F	S
1	2	3	4	5	6	7
8	9	10	11	12	13	14
15	16	17	18	19	20	21
22	23	24	25	26	27	28
29	30	31				

NOVEMBER

S	M	T	W	T	F	S
			1	2	3	4
5	6	7	8	9	10	11
12	13	14	15	16	17	18
19	20	21	22	23	24	25
26	27	28	29	30		

DECEMBER

S	M	T	W	T	F	S
					1	2
3	4	5	6	7	8	9
10	11	12	13	14	15	16
17	18	19	20	21	22	23
24	25	26	27	28	29	30
31						

2024

JANUARY

S	M	T	W	T	F	S
	1	2	3	4	5	6
7	8	9	10	11	12	13
14	15	16	17	18	19	20
21	22	23	24	25	26	27
28	29	30	31			

FEBRUARY

S	M	T	W	T	F	S
				1	2	3
4	5	6	7	8	9	10
11	12	13	14	15	16	17
18	19	20	21	22	23	24
25	26	27	28	29		

MARCH

S	M	T	W	T	F	S
					1	2
3	4	5	6	7	8	9
10	11	12	13	14	15	16
17	18	19	20	21	22	23
24	25	26	27	28	29	30
31						

APRIL

S	M	T	W	T	F	S
	1	2	3	4	5	6
7	8	9	10	11	12	13
14	15	16	17	18	19	20
21	22	23	24	25	26	27
28	29	30				

MAY

S	M	T	W	T	F	S
			1	2	3	4
5	6	7	8	9	10	11
12	13	14	15	16	17	18
19	20	21	22	23	24	25
26	27	28	29	30	31	

JUNE

S	M	T	W	T	F	S
						1
2	3	4	5	6	7	8
9	10	11	12	13	14	15
16	17	18	19	20	21	22
23	24	25	26	27	28	29
30						

JULY

S	M	T	W	T	F	S
	1	2	3	4	5	6
7	8	9	10	11	12	13
14	15	16	17	18	19	20
21	22	23	24	25	26	27
28	29	30	31			

AUGUST

S	M	T	W	T	F	S
				1	2	3
4	5	6	7	8	9	10
11	12	13	14	15	16	17
18	19	20	21	22	23	24
25	26	27	28	29	30	31

SEPTEMBER

S	M	T	W	T	F	S
1	2	3	4	5	6	7
8	9	10	11	12	13	14
15	16	17	18	19	20	21
22	23	24	25	26	27	28
29	30					

OCTOBER

S	M	T	W	T	F	S
		1	2	3	4	5
6	7	8	9	10	11	12
13	14	15	16	17	18	19
20	21	22	23	24	25	26
27	28	29	30	31		

NOVEMBER

S	M	T	W	T	F	S
					1	2
3	4	5	6	7	8	9
10	11	12	13	14	15	16
17	18	19	20	21	22	23
24	25	26	27	28	29	30

DECEMBER

S	M	T	W	T	F	S
1	2	3	4	5	6	7
8	9	10	11	12	13	14
15	16	17	18	19	20	21
22	23	24	25	26	27	28
29	30	31				

August

SUNDAY	MONDAY	TUESDAY	WEDNESDAY
	1 *Summer Bank Holiday (SCT)*	2	3
7	8	9	10
14	15	16	17
21	22	23	24
28	29 *Summer Bank Holiday (UK except SCT)*	30	31

2022

THURSDAY	FRIDAY	SATURDAY
4	5	6
11	12	13
18	19	20
25	26	27

July 2022

S	M	T	W	T	F	S
					1	2
3	4	5	6	7	8	9
10	11	12	13	14	15	16
17	18	19	20	21	22	23
24/31	25	26	27	28	29	30

September 2022

S	M	T	W	T	F	S
				1	2	3
4	5	6	7	8	9	10
11	12	13	14	15	16	17
18	19	20	21	22	23	24
25	26	27	28	29	30	

Projects

Grocery

Other things may change us, but we start and end with the family.

—Anthony Brandt

To do

August 2022

S	M	T	W	T	F	S
	1	2	3	4	5	6
7	8	9	10	11	12	13
14	15	16	17	18	19	20
21	22	23	24	25	26	27
28	29	30	31			

September 2022

S	M	T	W	T	F	S
				1	2	3
4	5	6	7	8	9	10
11	12	13	14	15	16	17
18	19	20	21	22	23	24
25	26	27	28	29	30	

2022 August

MONDAY *Summer Bank Holiday (SCT)*
1

TUESDAY
2

WEDNESDAY
3

THURSDAY
4

FRIDAY *First Quarter Moon*
5

SATURDAY
6

SUNDAY
7

Menus

Grocery

I think that's a real key to success in life, to not worry about the landing but enjoy the experience.

—Jennifer Aniston

To do

August 2022

S	M	T	W	T	F	S
	1	2	3	4	5	6
7	8	9	10	11	12	13
14	15	16	17	18	19	20
21	22	23	24	25	26	27
28	29	30	31			

September 2022

S	M	T	W	T	F	S
				1	2	3
4	5	6	7	8	9	10
11	12	13	14	15	16	17
18	19	20	21	22	23	24
25	26	27	28	29	30	

2022 August

MONDAY
8

TUESDAY
9

WEDNESDAY
10

THURSDAY
11

Full Moon

FRIDAY
12

SATURDAY
13

SUNDAY
14

Menus

Grocery

There's more to life than you know, and it's all happening out there. Discover what part you can play and then go for it.

—Sir Ian McKellen

To do

August 2022

S	M	T	W	T	F	S
	1	2	3	4	5	6
7	8	9	10	11	12	13
14	15	16	17	18	19	20
21	22	23	24	25	26	27
28	29	30	31			

September 2022

S	M	T	W	T	F	S
				1	2	3
4	5	6	7	8	9	10
11	12	13	14	15	16	17
18	19	20	21	22	23	24
25	26	27	28	29	30	

2022 August

MONDAY
15

TUESDAY
16

WEDNESDAY
17

THURSDAY
18

FRIDAY
19
Last Quarter Moon

SATURDAY
20

SUNDAY
21

Menus

Grocery

Optimism is the faith that leads to achievement; nothing can be done without hope.

—*Helen Keller*

To do

August 2022

S	M	T	W	T	F	S
	1	2	3	4	5	6
7	8	9	10	11	12	13
14	15	16	17	18	19	20
21	22	23	24	25	26	27
28	29	30	31			

September 2022

S	M	T	W	T	F	S
				1	2	3
4	5	6	7	8	9	10
11	12	13	14	15	16	17
18	19	20	21	22	23	24
25	26	27	28	29	30	

2022 August

MONDAY
22

TUESDAY
23

WEDNESDAY
24

THURSDAY
25

FRIDAY
26

SATURDAY *New Moon*
27

SUNDAY
28

Menus

September

SUNDAY	MONDAY	TUESDAY	WEDNESDAY
August 2022 (see below)	October 2022 (see below)		
4 *Father's Day (AUS, NZ)*	5 *Labor Day (USA, CAN)*	6	7
11 *Patriot Day*	12	13	14
18	19	20	21
25 *Rosh Hashanah begins*	26	27	28

August 2022

S	M	T	W	T	F	S
	1	2	3	4	5	6
7	8	9	10	11	12	13
14	15	16	17	18	19	20
21	22	23	24	25	26	27
28	29	30	31			

October 2022

S	M	T	W	T	F	S
						1
2	3	4	5	6	7	8
9	10	11	12	13	14	15
16	17	18	19	20	21	22
23/30	24/31	25	26	27	28	29

2022

THURSDAY	FRIDAY	SATURDAY
1	2	3
8	9	10
15	16	17
22	23 *Autumn begins (Northern Hemisphere)*	24
29	30	

Projects

Grocery

If you can dream it, you can do it.

—Walt Disney

To do

September 2022

S	M	T	W	T	F	S
				1	2	3
4	5	6	7	8	9	10
11	12	13	14	15	16	17
18	19	20	21	22	23	24
25	26	27	28	29	30	

October 2022

S	M	T	W	T	F	S
						1
2	3	4	5	6	7	8
9	10	11	12	13	14	15
16	17	18	19	20	21	22
23/30	24/31	25	26	27	28	29

2022 Aug./September

MONDAY *Summer Bank Holiday (UK except SCT)*
29

TUESDAY
30

WEDNESDAY
31

THURSDAY
1

FRIDAY
2

SATURDAY *First Quarter Moon*
3

SUNDAY *Father's Day (AUS, NZ)*
4

Menus

Grocery

And have the courage to accept that you're not perfect, nothing is, and no one is—and that's OK.

—Katie Couric

To do

September 2022

S	M	T	W	T	F	S
				1	2	3
4	5	6	7	8	9	10
11	12	13	14	15	16	17
18	19	20	21	22	23	24
25	26	27	28	29	30	

October 2022

S	M	T	W	T	F	S
						1
2	3	4	5	6	7	8
9	10	11	12	13	14	15
16	17	18	19	20	21	22
23/30	24/31	25	26	27	28	29

2022 September

MONDAY
5
Labor Day (USA, CAN)

TUESDAY
6

WEDNESDAY
7

THURSDAY
8

FRIDAY
9

SATURDAY
10
Full Moon

SUNDAY
11
Patriot Day

Menus

Grocery

What we want in the future will only happen if we do it every day. So, kindness matters enormously. And empathy. Finding some point of connection.

—Gloria Steinem

To do

September 2022

S	M	T	W	T	F	S
				1	2	3
4	5	6	7	8	9	10
11	12	13	14	15	16	17
18	19	20	21	22	23	24
25	26	27	28	29	30	

October 2022

S	M	T	W	T	F	S
						1
2	3	4	5	6	7	8
9	10	11	12	13	14	15
16	17	18	19	20	21	22
23/30	24/31	25	26	27	28	29

2022 September

MONDAY
12

TUESDAY
13

WEDNESDAY
14

THURSDAY
15

FRIDAY
16

SATURDAY
17
Last Quarter Moon

SUNDAY
18

Menus

Grocery

And if it doesn't end up the way I imagined in my head, it'll be OK. I just have to go for it, because that's just simply who we are now.

—Allyson Felix

To do

September 2022

S	M	T	W	T	F	S
				1	2	3
4	5	6	7	8	9	10
11	12	13	14	15	16	17
18	19	20	21	22	23	24
25	26	27	28	29	30	

October 2022

S	M	T	W	T	F	S
						1
2	3	4	5	6	7	8
9	10	11	12	13	14	15
16	17	18	19	20	21	22
23/30	24/31	25	26	27	28	29

2022 September

MONDAY
19

TUESDAY
20

WEDNESDAY
21

THURSDAY
22

FRIDAY
23
Autumn begins (Northern Hemisphere)

SATURDAY
24

SUNDAY
25
New Moon
Rosh Hashanah begins

Menus

Grocery

One of the greatest things in human life is the ability to make plans. Even if they never come true, the joy of anticipating is irrevocably yours. That way one can live many more than just one life.

—Maria von Trapp

To do

September 2022

S	M	T	W	T	F	S
				1	2	3
4	5	6	7	8	9	10
11	12	13	14	15	16	17
18	19	20	21	22	23	24
25	26	27	28	29	30	

October 2022

S	M	T	W	T	F	S
						1
2	3	4	5	6	7	8
9	10	11	12	13	14	15
16	17	18	19	20	21	22
23/30	24/31	25	26	27	28	29

2022 Sept./October

MONDAY
26

TUESDAY
27

WEDNESDAY
28

THURSDAY
29

FRIDAY
30

SATURDAY
1

SUNDAY *First Quarter Moon*
2

Menus

October

SUNDAY	MONDAY	TUESDAY	WEDNESDAY
September 2022 S M T W T F S 1 2 3 4 5 6 7 8 9 10 11 12 13 14 15 16 17 18 19 20 21 22 23 24 25 26 27 28 29 30	November 2022 S M T W T F S 1 2 3 4 5 6 7 8 9 10 11 12 13 14 15 16 17 18 19 20 21 22 23 24 25 26 27 28 29 30		
2	3	4 *Yom Kippur begins*	5
9 *Sukkot begins*	10 *Columbus Day (USA); Indigenous Peoples' Day (USA); Thanksgiving Day (CAN)*	11	12
16	17	18	19
23 / 30	24 *Diwali begins* / *Halloween* 31	25	26

THURSDAY	FRIDAY	SATURDAY
		1
6	7	8
13	14	15
20	21	22
27	28	29

Projects

Grocery

My mom said, "If you really want this, you're going to have to work really hard. Take advantage of every opportunity, and don't give up."

—Jane Goodall

To do

October 2022

S	M	T	W	T	F	S
						1
2	3	4	5	6	7	8
9	10	11	12	13	14	15
16	17	18	19	20	21	22
23/30	24/31	25	26	27	28	29

November 2022

S	M	T	W	T	F	S
		1	2	3	4	5
6	7	8	9	10	11	12
13	14	15	16	17	18	19
20	21	22	23	24	25	26
27	28	29	30			

2022 October

MONDAY
3

TUESDAY
4

Yom Kippur begins

WEDNESDAY
5

THURSDAY
6

FRIDAY
7

SATURDAY
8

SUNDAY
9

Full Moon
Sukkot begins

Menus

Grocery

Whatever happens to you belongs to you. Make it yours. Feed it to yourself even if it feels impossible to swallow. Let it nurture you, because it will.

—Cheryl Strayed

To do

October 2022

S	M	T	W	T	F	S
						1
2	3	4	5	6	7	8
9	10	11	12	13	14	15
16	17	18	19	20	21	22
23/30	24/31	25	26	27	28	29

November 2022

S	M	T	W	T	F	S
		1	2	3	4	5
6	7	8	9	10	11	12
13	14	15	16	17	18	19
20	21	22	23	24	25	26
27	28	29	30			

2022 October

MONDAY
10

Columbus Day (USA)
Indigenous Peoples' Day (USA)
Thanksgiving Day (CAN)

TUESDAY
11

WEDNESDAY
12

THURSDAY
13

FRIDAY
14

SATURDAY
15

SUNDAY
16

Menus

Grocery

If you're offered a seat on a rocket ship, don't ask what seat. Just get on.

—Sheryl Sandberg

To do

October 2022

S	M	T	W	T	F	S
						1
2	3	4	5	6	7	8
9	10	11	12	13	14	15
16	17	18	19	20	21	22
23/30	24/31	25	26	27	28	29

November 2022

S	M	T	W	T	F	S
		1	2	3	4	5
6	7	8	9	10	11	12
13	14	15	16	17	18	19
20	21	22	23	24	25	26
27	28	29	30			

2022 October

MONDAY
17

Last Quarter Moon

TUESDAY
18

WEDNESDAY
19

THURSDAY
20

FRIDAY
21

SATURDAY
22

SUNDAY
23

Menus

Grocery

Never give in—never, never, never, never, in nothing great or small, large or petty—never give in except to convictions of honor and good sense.

—Winston Churchill

To do

October 2022

S	M	T	W	T	F	S
						1
2	3	4	5	6	7	8
9	10	11	12	13	14	15
16	17	18	19	20	21	22
23/30	24/31	25	26	27	28	29

November 2022

S	M	T	W	T	F	S
		1	2	3	4	5
6	7	8	9	10	11	12
13	14	15	16	17	18	19
20	21	22	23	24	25	26
27	28	29	30			

2022 October

MONDAY *Diwali begins*
24

TUESDAY *New Moon*
25

WEDNESDAY
26

THURSDAY
27

FRIDAY
28

SATURDAY
29

SUNDAY
30

Menus

November

SUNDAY	MONDAY	TUESDAY	WEDNESDAY
		1	2
6 *Daylight Saving Time ends (USA, CAN)*	7	8 *Election Day*	9
13	14	15	16
20	21	22	23
27	28	29	30 *St. Andrew's Day (SCT)*

THURSDAY	FRIDAY	SATURDAY
3	4	5
10	11 *Veterans Day (USA); Remembrance Day (CAN, UK)*	12
17	18	19
24 *Thanksgiving Day*	25	26

October 2022

S	M	T	W	T	F	S
						1
2	3	4	5	6	7	8
9	10	11	12	13	14	15
16	17	18	19	20	21	22
23/30	24/31	25	26	27	28	29

December 2022

S	M	T	W	T	F	S
				1	2	3
4	5	6	7	8	9	10
11	12	13	14	15	16	17
18	19	20	21	22	23	24
25	26	27	28	29	30	31

Projects

Grocery

When you really don't know what to do—what do you do? How do you do it? You just put one foot in front of the other. You just do the next right thing.

—Kristen Bell

To do

November 2022

S	M	T	W	T	F	S
		1	2	3	4	5
6	7	8	9	10	11	12
13	14	15	16	17	18	19
20	21	22	23	24	25	26
27	28	29	30			

December 2022

S	M	T	W	T	F	S
				1	2	3
4	5	6	7	8	9	10
11	12	13	14	15	16	17
18	19	20	21	22	23	24
25	26	27	28	29	30	31

2022 Oct./November

MONDAY
31
Halloween

TUESDAY
1
First Quarter Moon

WEDNESDAY
2

THURSDAY
3

FRIDAY
4

SATURDAY
5

SUNDAY
6
Daylight Saving Time ends (USA, CAN)

Menus

Grocery

A journey of a thousand miles begins with a single step.

—Laozi

To do

November 2022

S	M	T	W	T	F	S
		1	2	3	4	5
6	7	8	9	10	11	12
13	14	15	16	17	18	19
20	21	22	23	24	25	26
27	28	29	30			

December 2022

S	M	T	W	T	F	S
				1	2	3
4	5	6	7	8	9	10
11	12	13	14	15	16	17
18	19	20	21	22	23	24
25	26	27	28	29	30	31

2022 November

MONDAY
7

TUESDAY
8

Full Moon
Election Day

WEDNESDAY
9

THURSDAY
10

FRIDAY
11

Veterans Day (USA)
Remembrance Day (CAN, UK)

SATURDAY
12

SUNDAY
13

Menus

Grocery

Each moment and whatever happens thrills me with joy.

—Walt Whitman, "Song of Myself"

To do

November 2022

S	M	T	W	T	F	S
		1	2	3	4	5
6	7	8	9	10	11	12
13	14	15	16	17	18	19
20	21	22	23	24	25	26
27	28	29	30			

December 2022

S	M	T	W	T	F	S
				1	2	3
4	5	6	7	8	9	10
11	12	13	14	15	16	17
18	19	20	21	22	23	24
25	26	27	28	29	30	31

2022 November

MONDAY
14

TUESDAY
15

WEDNESDAY
16
Last Quarter Moon

THURSDAY
17

FRIDAY
18

SATURDAY
19

SUNDAY
20

Menus

Grocery

Happiness is when what you think, what you say, and what you do are in harmony.

—Mahatma Gandhi

To do

November 2022

S	M	T	W	T	F	S
		1	2	3	4	5
6	7	8	9	10	11	12
13	14	15	16	17	18	19
20	21	22	23	24	25	26
27	28	29	30			

December 2022

S	M	T	W	T	F	S
				1	2	3
4	5	6	7	8	9	10
11	12	13	14	15	16	17
18	19	20	21	22	23	24
25	26	27	28	29	30	31

2022 November

MONDAY
21

TUESDAY
22

WEDNESDAY
New Moon
23

THURSDAY
Thanksgiving Day
24

FRIDAY
25

SATURDAY
26

SUNDAY
27

Menus

December

SUNDAY	MONDAY	TUESDAY	WEDNESDAY
November 2022 S M T W T F S 1 2 3 4 5 6 7 8 9 10 11 12 13 14 15 16 17 18 19 20 21 22 23 24 25 26 27 28 29 30	January 2023 S M T W T F S 1 2 3 4 5 6 7 8 9 10 11 12 13 14 15 16 17 18 19 20 21 22 23 24 25 26 27 28 29 30 31		
4	5	6	7 *Pearl Harbor Day*
11	12	13	14
18 *Hanukkah begins*	19	20	21 *Winter begins (Northern Hemisphere)*
25 *Christmas Day*	26 *Kwanzaa begins; Boxing Day (AUS, CAN, NZ, UK)*	27	28

2022

THURSDAY	FRIDAY	SATURDAY
1	2	3
8	9	10
15	16	17
22	23	24 *Christmas Eve*
29	30	31 *New Year's Eve*

Projects

Grocery

You are the one that possesses the keys to your being. You carry the passport to your own happiness.

—Diane von Furstenberg

To do

December 2022

S	M	T	W	T	F	S
				1	2	3
4	5	6	7	8	9	10
11	12	13	14	15	16	17
18	19	20	21	22	23	24
25	26	27	28	29	30	31

January 2023

S	M	T	W	T	F	S
1	2	3	4	5	6	7
8	9	10	11	12	13	14
15	16	17	18	19	20	21
22	23	24	25	26	27	28
29	30	31				

2022 Nov./December

MONDAY
28

TUESDAY
29

WEDNESDAY
30

First Quarter Moon
St. Andrew's Day (SCT)

THURSDAY
1

FRIDAY
2

SATURDAY
3

SUNDAY
4

Menus

Grocery

One of the secrets to staying young is to always do things you don't know how to do, to keep learning.

—Ruth Reichl

To do

December 2022

S	M	T	W	T	F	S
				1	2	3
4	5	6	7	8	9	10
11	12	13	14	15	16	17
18	19	20	21	22	23	24
25	26	27	28	29	30	31

January 2023

S	M	T	W	T	F	S
1	2	3	4	5	6	7
8	9	10	11	12	13	14
15	16	17	18	19	20	21
22	23	24	25	26	27	28
29	30	31				

2022 December

MONDAY
5

TUESDAY
6

WEDNESDAY
7

Full Moon
Pearl Harbor Day

THURSDAY
8

FRIDAY
9

SATURDAY
10

SUNDAY
11

Menus

Grocery

One's life has value so long as one attributes value to the life of others, by means of love, friendship, indignation, compassion.

—Simone de Beauvoir

To do

December 2022

S	M	T	W	T	F	S
				1	2	3
4	5	6	7	8	9	10
11	12	13	14	15	16	17
18	19	20	21	22	23	24
25	26	27	28	29	30	31

January 2023

S	M	T	W	T	F	S
1	2	3	4	5	6	7
8	9	10	11	12	13	14
15	16	17	18	19	20	21
22	23	24	25	26	27	28
29	30	31				

2022 December

MONDAY
12

TUESDAY
13

WEDNESDAY
14

THURSDAY
15

FRIDAY
16

Last Quarter Moon

SATURDAY
17

SUNDAY
18

Hanukkah begins

Menus

Grocery

We must have perseverance and above all confidence in ourselves. We must believe that we are gifted for something and that this thing, at whatever cost, must be attained.

—Marie Curie

To do

December 2022

S	M	T	W	T	F	S
				1	2	3
4	5	6	7	8	9	10
11	12	13	14	15	16	17
18	19	20	21	22	23	24
25	26	27	28	29	30	31

January 2023

S	M	T	W	T	F	S
1	2	3	4	5	6	7
8	9	10	11	12	13	14
15	16	17	18	19	20	21
22	23	24	25	26	27	28
29	30	31				

2022 December

MONDAY
19

TUESDAY
20

WEDNESDAY *Winter begins (Northern Hemisphere)*
21

THURSDAY
22

FRIDAY *New Moon*
23

SATURDAY *Christmas Eve*
24

SUNDAY *Christmas Day*
25

Menus

Grocery

You are not your circumstances. You are your possibilities. If you know that, you can do anything.

—Oprah Winfrey

To do

December 2022

S	M	T	W	T	F	S
				1	2	3
4	5	6	7	8	9	10
11	12	13	14	15	16	17
18	19	20	21	22	23	24
25	26	27	28	29	30	31

January 2023

S	M	T	W	T	F	S
1	2	3	4	5	6	7
8	9	10	11	12	13	14
15	16	17	18	19	20	21
22	23	24	25	26	27	28
29	30	31				

2022/23 Dec./January

MONDAY
26
Kwanzaa begins
Boxing Day (AUS, CAN, NZ, UK)

TUESDAY
27

WEDNESDAY
28

THURSDAY
29
First Quarter Moon

FRIDAY
30

SATURDAY
31
New Year's Eve

SUNDAY
1
New Year's Day

Menus

January

SUNDAY	MONDAY	TUESDAY	WEDNESDAY
1 *New Year's Day*	2 *Day after New Year's Day (NZ, SCT)*	3	4
8	9	10	11
15	16 *Martin Luther King Jr. Day*	17	18
22 *Chinese New Year*	23	24	25
29	30	31	

2023

THURSDAY	FRIDAY	SATURDAY
5	6	7
12	13	14
19	20	21
26 *Australia Day (AUS)*	27	28

December 2022

S	M	T	W	T	F	S
				1	2	3
4	5	6	7	8	9	10
11	12	13	14	15	16	17
18	19	20	21	22	23	24
25	26	27	28	29	30	31

February 2023

S	M	T	W	T	F	S
			1	2	3	4
5	6	7	8	9	10	11
12	13	14	15	16	17	18
19	20	21	22	23	24	25
26	27	28				

Projects

Grocery

Lead by example with hope, never fear.

—Michelle Obama

To do

January 2023

S	M	T	W	T	F	S
1	2	3	4	5	6	7
8	9	10	11	12	13	14
15	16	17	18	19	20	21
22	23	24	25	26	27	28
29	30	31				

February 2023

S	M	T	W	T	F	S
			1	2	3	4
5	6	7	8	9	10	11
12	13	14	15	16	17	18
19	20	21	22	23	24	25
26	27	28				

2023 January

MONDAY *Day after New Year's Day (NZ, SCT)*

2

TUESDAY

3

WEDNESDAY

4

THURSDAY

5

FRIDAY *Full Moon*

6

SATURDAY

7

SUNDAY

8

Menus

Grocery

Let us all be the leaders we wish we had.

—Simon Sinek

To do

January 2023

S	M	T	W	T	F	S
1	2	3	4	5	6	7
8	9	10	11	12	13	14
15	16	17	18	19	20	21
22	23	24	25	26	27	28
29	30	31				

February 2023

S	M	T	W	T	F	S
			1	2	3	4
5	6	7	8	9	10	11
12	13	14	15	16	17	18
19	20	21	22	23	24	25
26	27	28				

2023 January

MONDAY
9

TUESDAY
10

WEDNESDAY
11

THURSDAY
12

FRIDAY
13

SATURDAY
14

SUNDAY *Last Quarter Moon*
15

Menus

Grocery

The purpose of life...is to live it, to taste experience to the utmost, to reach out eagerly and without fear for newer and richer experience.

—Eleanor Roosevelt

To do

January 2023

S	M	T	W	T	F	S
1	2	3	4	5	6	7
8	9	10	11	12	13	14
15	16	17	18	19	20	21
22	23	24	25	26	27	28
29	30	31				

February 2023

S	M	T	W	T	F	S
			1	2	3	4
5	6	7	8	9	10	11
12	13	14	15	16	17	18
19	20	21	22	23	24	25
26	27	28				

2023 January

MONDAY *Martin Luther King Jr. Day*

16

TUESDAY

17

WEDNESDAY

18

THURSDAY

19

FRIDAY

20

SATURDAY *New Moon*

21

SUNDAY *Chinese New Year*

22

Menus

Grocery

The achievement of happiness requires not the... satisfaction of our needs...but the examination and transformation of those needs.

—Stanley Cavell

To do

January 2023

S	M	T	W	T	F	S
1	2	3	4	5	6	7
8	9	10	11	12	13	14
15	16	17	18	19	20	21
22	23	24	25	26	27	28
29	30	31				

February 2023

S	M	T	W	T	F	S
			1	2	3	4
5	6	7	8	9	10	11
12	13	14	15	16	17	18
19	20	21	22	23	24	25
26	27	28				

2023 January

MONDAY
23

TUESDAY
24

WEDNESDAY
25

THURSDAY
26
Australia Day (AUS)

FRIDAY
27

SATURDAY
28
First Quarter Moon

SUNDAY
29

Menus

February

SUNDAY	MONDAY	TUESDAY	WEDNESDAY
			1
5	6 *Waitangi Day (NZ)*	7	8
12 *Abraham Lincoln's Birthday*	13	14 *Valentine's Day*	15
19	20 *Presidents' Day*	21	22 *Ash Wednesday (Lent begins)*
26	27	28	

2023

THURSDAY	FRIDAY	SATURDAY
2 *Groundhog Day*	3	4
9	10	11
16	17	18
23	24	25

January 2023

S	M	T	W	T	F	S
1	2	3	4	5	6	7
8	9	10	11	12	13	14
15	16	17	18	19	20	21
22	23	24	25	26	27	28
29	30	31				

March 2023

S	M	T	W	T	F	S
			1	2	3	4
5	6	7	8	9	10	11
12	13	14	15	16	17	18
19	20	21	22	23	24	25
26	27	28	29	30	31	

Projects

Grocery

Do your little bit of good where you are; it's those little bits of good that overwhelm the world.

—Desmond Tutu

To do

February 2023

S	M	T	W	T	F	S
			1	2	3	4
5	6	7	8	9	10	11
12	13	14	15	16	17	18
19	20	21	22	23	24	25
26	27	28				

March 2023

S	M	T	W	T	F	S
			1	2	3	4
5	6	7	8	9	10	11
12	13	14	15	16	17	18
19	20	21	22	23	24	25
26	27	28	29	30	31	

2023 Jan./February

MONDAY
30

TUESDAY
31

WEDNESDAY
1

THURSDAY *Groundhog Day*
2

FRIDAY
3

SATURDAY
4

SUNDAY *Full Moon*
5

Menus

Grocery

We all have ability. The difference is how we use it.

—Stevie Wonder

To do

February 2023

S	M	T	W	T	F	S
			1	2	3	4
5	6	7	8	9	10	11
12	13	14	15	16	17	18
19	20	21	22	23	24	25
26	27	28				

March 2023

S	M	T	W	T	F	S
			1	2	3	4
5	6	7	8	9	10	11
12	13	14	15	16	17	18
19	20	21	22	23	24	25
26	27	28	29	30	31	

2023 February

MONDAY *Waitangi Day (NZ)*

6

TUESDAY

7

WEDNESDAY

8

THURSDAY

9

FRIDAY

10

SATURDAY

11

SUNDAY *Abraham Lincoln's Birthday*

12

Menus

Grocery

I find ecstasy in living; the mere sense of living is joy enough.

—Emily Dickinson

To do

February 2023

S	M	T	W	T	F	S
			1	2	3	4
5	6	7	8	9	10	11
12	13	14	15	16	17	18
19	20	21	22	23	24	25
26	27	28				

March 2023

S	M	T	W	T	F	S
			1	2	3	4
5	6	7	8	9	10	11
12	13	14	15	16	17	18
19	20	21	22	23	24	25
26	27	28	29	30	31	

2023 February

MONDAY *Last Quarter Moon*
13

TUESDAY *Valentine's Day*
14

WEDNESDAY
15

THURSDAY
16

FRIDAY
17

SATURDAY
18

SUNDAY
19

Menus

Grocery

The good life is one inspired by love and guided by knowledge.

—Bertrand Russell

To do

February 2023

S	M	T	W	T	F	S
			1	2	3	4
5	6	7	8	9	10	11
12	13	14	15	16	17	18
19	20	21	22	23	24	25
26	27	28				

March 2023

S	M	T	W	T	F	S
			1	2	3	4
5	6	7	8	9	10	11
12	13	14	15	16	17	18
19	20	21	22	23	24	25
26	27	28	29	30	31	

2023 February

MONDAY
20

New Moon
Presidents' Day

TUESDAY
21

WEDNESDAY
22

Ash Wednesday (Lent begins)

THURSDAY
23

FRIDAY
24

SATURDAY
25

SUNDAY
26

Menus

March

SUNDAY	MONDAY	TUESDAY	WEDNESDAY
February 2023 S M T W T F S 1 2 3 4 5 6 7 8 9 10 11 12 13 14 15 16 17 18 19 20 21 22 23 24 25 26 27 28	April 2023 S M T W T F S 1 2 3 4 5 6 7 8 9 10 11 12 13 14 15 16 17 18 19 20 21 22 23/30 24 25 26 27 28 29		1
5	6 *Purim begins*	7	8 *International Women's Day*
12 *Daylight Saving Time begins (USA, CAN)*	13 *Public Holiday (AUS: ACT, SA, TAS, VIC)*	14	15
19 *Mothering Sunday (UK)*	20 *Spring begins (Northern Hemisphere)*	21	22 *Ramadan begins*
26	27	28	29

2023

THURSDAY	FRIDAY	SATURDAY
2	3	4
9	10	11
16	17 St. Patrick's Day	18
23	24	25
30	31	

Projects

Grocery

What necessity is there to dwell on the Past, when the Present is so much surer—the Future so much brighter?

—*Charlotte Brontë,* Jane Eyre

To do

March 2023

S	M	T	W	T	F	S
			1	2	3	4
5	6	7	8	9	10	11
12	13	14	15	16	17	18
19	20	21	22	23	24	25
26	27	28	29	30	31	

April 2023

S	M	T	W	T	F	S
						1
2	3	4	5	6	7	8
9	10	11	12	13	14	15
16	17	18	19	20	21	22
23/30	24	25	26	27	28	29

2023 February/March

MONDAY
27
First Quarter Moon

TUESDAY
28

WEDNESDAY
1

THURSDAY
2

FRIDAY
3

SATURDAY
4

SUNDAY
5

Menus

Grocery

I'm so thankful for friendship. It beautifies life so much.

—Lucy Maud Montgomery, Anne of Avonlea

To do

March 2023

S	M	T	W	T	F	S
			1	2	3	4
5	6	7	8	9	10	11
12	13	14	15	16	17	18
19	20	21	22	23	24	25
26	27	28	29	30	31	

April 2023

S	M	T	W	T	F	S
						1
2	3	4	5	6	7	8
9	10	11	12	13	14	15
16	17	18	19	20	21	22
23/30	24	25	26	27	28	29

2023 March

MONDAY *Purim begins*

6

TUESDAY *Full Moon*

7

WEDNESDAY *International Women's Day*

8

THURSDAY

9

FRIDAY

10

SATURDAY

11

SUNDAY *Daylight Saving Time begins (USA, CAN)*

12

Menus

Grocery

All things are ready if our minds be so.

—William Shakespeare, Henry V

To do

March 2023

S	M	T	W	T	F	S
			1	2	3	4
5	6	7	8	9	10	11
12	13	14	15	16	17	18
19	20	21	22	23	24	25
26	27	28	29	30	31	

April 2023

S	M	T	W	T	F	S
						1
2	3	4	5	6	7	8
9	10	11	12	13	14	15
16	17	18	19	20	21	22
23/30	24	25	26	27	28	29

2023 March

MONDAY
13
Public Holiday (AUS: ACT, SA, TAS, VIC)

TUESDAY
14

WEDNESDAY
15
Last Quarter Moon

THURSDAY
16

FRIDAY
17
St. Patrick's Day

SATURDAY
18

SUNDAY
19
Mothering Sunday (UK)

Menus

Grocery

Love begins at home.

—Mother Teresa

To do

March 2023

S	M	T	W	T	F	S
			1	2	3	4
5	6	7	8	9	10	11
12	13	14	15	16	17	18
19	20	21	22	23	24	25
26	27	28	29	30	31	

April 2023

S	M	T	W	T	F	S
						1
2	3	4	5	6	7	8
9	10	11	12	13	14	15
16	17	18	19	20	21	22
23/30	24	25	26	27	28	29

2023 March

MONDAY *Spring begins (Northern Hemisphere)*
20

TUESDAY *New Moon*
21

WEDNESDAY *Ramadan begins*
22

THURSDAY
23

FRIDAY
24

SATURDAY
25

SUNDAY
26

Menus

Grocery

When I dare to be powerful, to use my strength in service of my vision, then it becomes less and less important whether I am afraid.

—Audre Lorde

To do

March 2023

S	M	T	W	T	F	S
			1	2	3	4
5	6	7	8	9	10	11
12	13	14	15	16	17	18
19	20	21	22	23	24	25
26	27	28	29	30	31	

April 2023

S	M	T	W	T	F	S
						1
2	3	4	5	6	7	8
9	10	11	12	13	14	15
16	17	18	19	20	21	22
23/30	24	25	26	27	28	29

2023 March/April

MONDAY
27

TUESDAY
28

WEDNESDAY *First Quarter Moon*
29

THURSDAY
30

FRIDAY
31

SATURDAY *April Fools' Day*
1

SUNDAY *Palm Sunday*
2

Menus

April

SUNDAY	MONDAY	TUESDAY	WEDNESDAY
March 2023 S M T W T F S 1 2 3 4 5 6 7 8 9 10 11 12 13 14 15 16 17 18 19 20 21 22 23 24 25 26 27 28 29 30 31	May 2023 S M T W T F S 1 2 3 4 5 6 7 8 9 10 11 12 13 14 15 16 17 18 19 20 21 22 23 24 25 26 27 28 29 30 31		
2 *Palm Sunday*	3	4	5 *Passover begins*
9 *Easter*	10 *Easter Monday (AUS, CAN, NZ, UK except SCT)*	11	12
16	17	18 *Tax Day*	19
23 / 30	24	25 *Anzac Day (AUS, NZ)*	26

2023

THURSDAY	FRIDAY	SATURDAY
		1 *April Fools' Day*
6	7 *Good Friday*	8
13	14	15
20	21 *Eid al-Fitr begins*	22 *Earth Day*
27	28 *Workers' Memorial Day (UK)*	29

Projects

Grocery

Make each day your masterpiece.

—John Wooden

To do

April 2023

S	M	T	W	T	F	S
						1
2	3	4	5	6	7	8
9	10	11	12	13	14	15
16	17	18	19	20	21	22
23/30	24	25	26	27	28	29

May 2023

S	M	T	W	T	F	S
	1	2	3	4	5	6
7	8	9	10	11	12	13
14	15	16	17	18	19	20
21	22	23	24	25	26	27
28	29	30	31			

2023 April

MONDAY
3

TUESDAY
4

WEDNESDAY
5
Passover begins

THURSDAY
6
Full Moon

FRIDAY
7
Good Friday

SATURDAY
8

SUNDAY
9
Easter

Menus

Grocery

Nothing is a waste of time if you use the experience wisely.

—Auguste Rodin

To do

April 2023

S	M	T	W	T	F	S
						1
2	3	4	5	6	7	8
9	10	11	12	13	14	15
16	17	18	19	20	21	22
23/30	24	25	26	27	28	29

May 2023

S	M	T	W	T	F	S
	1	2	3	4	5	6
7	8	9	10	11	12	13
14	15	16	17	18	19	20
21	22	23	24	25	26	27
28	29	30	31			

2023 April

MONDAY *Easter Monday (AUS, CAN, NZ, UK except SCT)*
10

TUESDAY
11

WEDNESDAY
12

THURSDAY *Last Quarter Moon*
13

FRIDAY
14

SATURDAY
15

SUNDAY
16

Menus

Grocery

I have a heart with room for every joy.

—Philip James Bailey

To do

April 2023

S	M	T	W	T	F	S
						1
2	3	4	5	6	7	8
9	10	11	12	13	14	15
16	17	18	19	20	21	22
23/30	24	25	26	27	28	29

May 2023

S	M	T	W	T	F	S
	1	2	3	4	5	6
7	8	9	10	11	12	13
14	15	16	17	18	19	20
21	22	23	24	25	26	27
28	29	30	31			

2023 April

MONDAY
17

TUESDAY
18
Tax Day

WEDNESDAY
19

THURSDAY
20
New Moon

FRIDAY
21
Eid al-Fitr begins

SATURDAY
22
Earth Day

SUNDAY
23

Menus

Grocery

It is better to fail in originality than to succeed in imitation.

—Herman Melville

To do

April 2023

S	M	T	W	T	F	S
						1
2	3	4	5	6	7	8
9	10	11	12	13	14	15
16	17	18	19	20	21	22
23/30	24	25	26	27	28	29

May 2023

S	M	T	W	T	F	S
	1	2	3	4	5	6
7	8	9	10	11	12	13
14	15	16	17	18	19	20
21	22	23	24	25	26	27
28	29	30	31			

2023 April

MONDAY
24

TUESDAY
25
Anzac Day (AUS, NZ)

WEDNESDAY
26

THURSDAY
27
First Quarter Moon

FRIDAY
28
Workers' Memorial Day (UK)

SATURDAY
29

SUNDAY
30

Menus

May

SUNDAY	MONDAY	TUESDAY	WEDNESDAY
	1	2	3
7	8	9	10
14 *Mother's Day (USA, AUS, CAN, NZ)*	15	16	17
21	22 *Victoria Day (CAN)*	23	24
28	29 *Memorial Day (USA); Spring Bank Holiday (UK)*	30	31

2023

THURSDAY	FRIDAY	SATURDAY
4	5 *Cinco de Mayo*	6
11	12	13
18	19	20 *Armed Forces Day*
25 *Shavuot begins*	26	27

April 2023

S	M	T	W	T	F	S
						1
2	3	4	5	6	7	8
9	10	11	12	13	14	15
16	17	18	19	20	21	22
23/30	24	25	26	27	28	29

June 2023

S	M	T	W	T	F	S
				1	2	3
4	5	6	7	8	9	10
11	12	13	14	15	16	17
18	19	20	21	22	23	24
25	26	27	28	29	30	

Projects

Grocery

Humor is your own unconscious therapy. Like a welcome summer rain, humor may suddenly cleanse and cool the earth, the air, and you.

—Langston Hughes

To do

May 2023

S	M	T	W	T	F	S
	1	2	3	4	5	6
7	8	9	10	11	12	13
14	15	16	17	18	19	20
21	22	23	24	25	26	27
28	29	30	31			

June 2023

S	M	T	W	T	F	S
				1	2	3
4	5	6	7	8	9	10
11	12	13	14	15	16	17
18	19	20	21	22	23	24
25	26	27	28	29	30	

2023 May

MONDAY
1

TUESDAY
2

WEDNESDAY
3

THURSDAY
4

FRIDAY
5

Full Moon
Cinco de Mayo

SATURDAY
6

SUNDAY
7

Menus

Grocery

You can't be that kid standing at the top of the waterslide, overthinking it. You have to go down the chute.

—Tina Fey

To do

May 2023

S	M	T	W	T	F	S
	1	2	3	4	5	6
7	8	9	10	11	12	13
14	15	16	17	18	19	20
21	22	23	24	25	26	27
28	29	30	31			

June 2023

S	M	T	W	T	F	S
				1	2	3
4	5	6	7	8	9	10
11	12	13	14	15	16	17
18	19	20	21	22	23	24
25	26	27	28	29	30	

2023 May

MONDAY
8

TUESDAY
9

WEDNESDAY
10

THURSDAY
11

FRIDAY *Last Quarter Moon*
12

SATURDAY
13

SUNDAY *Mother's Day (USA, AUS, CAN, NZ)*
14

Menus

Grocery

Decide...whether or not the goal is worth the risks involved. If it is, stop worrying.

—Amelia Earhart

To do

May 2023

S	M	T	W	T	F	S
	1	2	3	4	5	6
7	8	9	10	11	12	13
14	15	16	17	18	19	20
21	22	23	24	25	26	27
28	29	30	31			

June 2023

S	M	T	W	T	F	S
				1	2	3
4	5	6	7	8	9	10
11	12	13	14	15	16	17
18	19	20	21	22	23	24
25	26	27	28	29	30	

2023 May

MONDAY
15

TUESDAY
16

WEDNESDAY
17

THURSDAY
18

FRIDAY *New Moon*
19

SATURDAY *Armed Forces Day*
20

SUNDAY
21

Menus

Grocery

Setting goals is the first step in turning the invisible into the visible.

—Tony Robbins

To do

May 2023

S	M	T	W	T	F	S
	1	2	3	4	5	6
7	8	9	10	11	12	13
14	15	16	17	18	19	20
21	22	23	24	25	26	27
28	29	30	31			

June 2023

S	M	T	W	T	F	S
				1	2	3
4	5	6	7	8	9	10
11	12	13	14	15	16	17
18	19	20	21	22	23	24
25	26	27	28	29	30	

2023 May

MONDAY
22
Victoria Day (CAN)

TUESDAY
23

WEDNESDAY
24

THURSDAY
25
Shavuot begins

FRIDAY
26

SATURDAY
27
First Quarter Moon

SUNDAY
28

Menus

June

SUNDAY	MONDAY	TUESDAY	WEDNESDAY
May 2023 S M T W T F S 1 2 3 4 5 6 7 8 9 10 11 12 13 14 15 16 17 18 19 20 21 22 23 24 25 26 27 28 29 30 31	July 2023 S M T W T F S 1 2 3 4 5 6 7 8 9 10 11 12 13 14 15 16 17 18 19 20 21 22 23/30 24/31 25 26 27 28 29		
4	5	6	7
11	12	13	14 *Flag Day*
18 *Father's Day (USA, CAN, UK)*	19 *Juneteenth*	20	21 *Summer begins (Northern Hemisphere)*
25	26	27	28 *Eid al-Adha begins*

2023

THURSDAY	FRIDAY	SATURDAY
1	2	3
8	9	10
15	16	17
22	23	24
29	30	

Projects

Grocery

Courage starts with showing up and letting ourselves be seen.

—Brené Brown

To do

June 2023

S	M	T	W	T	F	S
				1	2	3
4	5	6	7	8	9	10
11	12	13	14	15	16	17
18	19	20	21	22	23	24
25	26	27	28	29	30	

July 2023

S	M	T	W	T	F	S
						1
2	3	4	5	6	7	8
9	10	11	12	13	14	15
16	17	18	19	20	21	22
23/30	24/31	25	26	27	28	29

2023 May/June

MONDAY
29
Memorial Day (USA)
Spring Bank Holiday (UK)

TUESDAY
30

WEDNESDAY
31

THURSDAY
1

FRIDAY
2

SATURDAY
3

SUNDAY
4
Full Moon

Menus

Grocery

If a little daydreaming is dangerous, the cure for it is not to dream less but to dream more, to dream all the time.

—Marcel Proust

To do

June 2023

S	M	T	W	T	F	S
				1	2	3
4	5	6	7	8	9	10
11	12	13	14	15	16	17
18	19	20	21	22	23	24
25	26	27	28	29	30	

July 2023

S	M	T	W	T	F	S
						1
2	3	4	5	6	7	8
9	10	11	12	13	14	15
16	17	18	19	20	21	22
23/30	24/31	25	26	27	28	29

2023 June

MONDAY
5

TUESDAY
6

WEDNESDAY
7

THURSDAY
8

FRIDAY
9

SATURDAY
10

Last Quarter Moon

SUNDAY
11

Menus

Grocery

The world will see you the way you see you, and treat you the way you treat yourself.

—Beyoncé

To do

June 2023

S	M	T	W	T	F	S
				1	2	3
4	5	6	7	8	9	10
11	12	13	14	15	16	17
18	19	20	21	22	23	24
25	26	27	28	29	30	

July 2023

S	M	T	W	T	F	S
						1
2	3	4	5	6	7	8
9	10	11	12	13	14	15
16	17	18	19	20	21	22
23/30	24/31	25	26	27	28	29

2023 June

MONDAY
12

TUESDAY
13

WEDNESDAY
14
Flag Day

THURSDAY
15

FRIDAY
16

SATURDAY
17

SUNDAY
18
New Moon
Father's Day (USA, CAN, UK)

Menus

Grocery

We know we must decide whether to stay small, quiet, and uncomplicated or allow ourselves to grow as big, loud, and complex as we were made to be.

—Glennon Doyle

To do

June 2023

S	M	T	W	T	F	S
				1	2	3
4	5	6	7	8	9	10
11	12	13	14	15	16	17
18	19	20	21	22	23	24
25	26	27	28	29	30	

July 2023

S	M	T	W	T	F	S
						1
2	3	4	5	6	7	8
9	10	11	12	13	14	15
16	17	18	19	20	21	22
23/30	24/31	25	26	27	28	29

2023 June

MONDAY *Juneteenth*

19

TUESDAY

20

WEDNESDAY *Summer begins (Northern Hemisphere)*

21

THURSDAY

22

FRIDAY

23

SATURDAY

24

SUNDAY

25

Menus

Grocery

Reflect upon your present blessings—of which every man has many—not on your past misfortunes, of which all men have some.

—*Charles Dickens,* Sketches by Boz

To do

June 2023

S	M	T	W	T	F	S
				1	2	3
4	5	6	7	8	9	10
11	12	13	14	15	16	17
18	19	20	21	22	23	24
25	26	27	28	29	30	

July 2023

S	M	T	W	T	F	S
						1
2	3	4	5	6	7	8
9	10	11	12	13	14	15
16	17	18	19	20	21	22
23/30	24/31	25	26	27	28	29

2023 June/July

MONDAY *First Quarter Moon*
26

TUESDAY
27

WEDNESDAY *Eid al-Adha begins*
28

THURSDAY
29

FRIDAY
30

SATURDAY *Canada Day (CAN)*
1

SUNDAY
2

Menus

July

SUNDAY	MONDAY	TUESDAY	WEDNESDAY
June 2023 S M T W T F S 1 2 3 4 5 6 7 8 9 10 11 12 13 14 15 16 17 18 19 20 21 22 23 24 25 26 27 28 29 30	August 2023 S M T W T F S 1 2 3 4 5 6 7 8 9 10 11 12 13 14 15 16 17 18 19 20 21 22 23 24 25 26 27 28 29 30 31		
2	3	4 *Independence Day*	5
9	10	11	12 *Orangemen's Day—Battle of the Boyne (NIR)*
16	17	18	19
23 / 30	24 / 31	25	26

2023

THURSDAY	FRIDAY	SATURDAY
		1 *Canada Day (CAN)*
6	7	8
13	14	15
20	21	22
27	28	29

Projects

Grocery

The ultimate measure of a man is not where he stands in moments of comfort and convenience but where he stands at times of challenge and controversy.

—Martin Luther King Jr.

To do

July 2023

S	M	T	W	T	F	S
						1
2	3	4	5	6	7	8
9	10	11	12	13	14	15
16	17	18	19	20	21	22
23/30	24/31	25	26	27	28	29

August 2023

S	M	T	W	T	F	S
		1	2	3	4	5
6	7	8	9	10	11	12
13	14	15	16	17	18	19
20	21	22	23	24	25	26
27	28	29	30	31		

2023 July

MONDAY *Full Moon*

3

TUESDAY *Independence Day*

4

WEDNESDAY

5

THURSDAY

6

FRIDAY

7

SATURDAY

8

SUNDAY

9

Menus

Grocery

When he has finished getting himself ready in the morning, he must go get the planet ready.

—*Antoine de Saint-Exupéry,* The Little Prince

To do

July 2023

S	M	T	W	T	F	S
						1
2	3	4	5	6	7	8
9	10	11	12	13	14	15
16	17	18	19	20	21	22
23/30	24/31	25	26	27	28	29

August 2023

S	M	T	W	T	F	S
		1	2	3	4	5
6	7	8	9	10	11	12
13	14	15	16	17	18	19
20	21	22	23	24	25	26
27	28	29	30	31		

2023 July

MONDAY *Last Quarter Moon*
10

TUESDAY
11

WEDNESDAY *Orangemen's Day—Battle of the Boyne (NIR)*
12

THURSDAY
13

FRIDAY
14

SATURDAY
15

SUNDAY
16

Menus

Grocery

Real change, enduring change, happens one step at a time.

—Ruth Bader Ginsburg

To do

July 2023

S	M	T	W	T	F	S
						1
2	3	4	5	6	7	8
9	10	11	12	13	14	15
16	17	18	19	20	21	22
23/30	24/31	25	26	27	28	29

August 2023

S	M	T	W	T	F	S
		1	2	3	4	5
6	7	8	9	10	11	12
13	14	15	16	17	18	19
20	21	22	23	24	25	26
27	28	29	30	31		

2023 July

MONDAY *New Moon*
17

TUESDAY
18

WEDNESDAY
19

THURSDAY
20

FRIDAY
21

SATURDAY
22

SUNDAY
23

Menus

Grocery

Carry out a random act of kindness with no expectation of reward, safe in the knowledge that one day, someone might do the same for you.

—Diana, Princess of Wales

To do

July 2023

S	M	T	W	T	F	S
						1
2	3	4	5	6	7	8
9	10	11	12	13	14	15
16	17	18	19	20	21	22
23/30	24/31	25	26	27	28	29

August 2023

S	M	T	W	T	F	S
		1	2	3	4	5
6	7	8	9	10	11	12
13	14	15	16	17	18	19
20	21	22	23	24	25	26
27	28	29	30	31		

2023 July

MONDAY
24

TUESDAY
25
First Quarter Moon

WEDNESDAY
26

THURSDAY
27

FRIDAY
28

SATURDAY
29

SUNDAY
30

Menus

August

SUNDAY	MONDAY	TUESDAY	WEDNESDAY
		1	2
6	7 *Summer Bank Holiday (SCT)*	8	9
13	14	15	16
20	21	22	23
27	28 *Summer Bank Holiday (UK except SCT)*	29	30

2023

THURSDAY	FRIDAY	SATURDAY
3	4	5
10	11	12
17	18	19
24	25	26
31		

July 2023

S	M	T	W	T	F	S
						1
2	3	4	5	6	7	8
9	10	11	12	13	14	15
16	17	18	19	20	21	22
23/30	24/31	25	26	27	28	29

September 2023

S	M	T	W	T	F	S
					1	2
3	4	5	6	7	8	9
10	11	12	13	14	15	16
17	18	19	20	21	22	23
24	25	26	27	28	29	30

Projects

Grocery

You must take life the way it comes at you and make the best of it.

—*Yann Martel,* Life of Pi

To do

August 2023

S	M	T	W	T	F	S
		1	2	3	4	5
6	7	8	9	10	11	12
13	14	15	16	17	18	19
20	21	22	23	24	25	26
27	28	29	30	31		

September 2023

S	M	T	W	T	F	S
					1	2
3	4	5	6	7	8	9
10	11	12	13	14	15	16
17	18	19	20	21	22	23
24	25	26	27	28	29	30

2023 July/August

MONDAY
31

TUESDAY
Full Moon
1

WEDNESDAY
2

THURSDAY
3

FRIDAY
4

SATURDAY
5

SUNDAY
6

Menus

Grocery

Helped are those who are content to be themselves; they will never lack mystery in their lives, and the joys of self-discovery will be constant.

—*Alice Walker,* The Temple of My Familiar

To do

August 2023

S	M	T	W	T	F	S
		1	2	3	4	5
6	7	8	9	10	11	12
13	14	15	16	17	18	19
20	21	22	23	24	25	26
27	28	29	30	31		

September 2023

S	M	T	W	T	F	S
					1	2
3	4	5	6	7	8	9
10	11	12	13	14	15	16
17	18	19	20	21	22	23
24	25	26	27	28	29	30

2023 August

MONDAY *Summer Bank Holiday (SCT)*

7

TUESDAY *Last Quarter Moon*

8

WEDNESDAY

9

THURSDAY

10

FRIDAY

11

SATURDAY

12

SUNDAY

13

Menus

Grocery

I can accept failure. Everyone fails at something. But I can't accept not trying.

—Michael Jordan

To do

August 2023

S	M	T	W	T	F	S
		1	2	3	4	5
6	7	8	9	10	11	12
13	14	15	16	17	18	19
20	21	22	23	24	25	26
27	28	29	30	31		

September 2023

S	M	T	W	T	F	S
					1	2
3	4	5	6	7	8	9
10	11	12	13	14	15	16
17	18	19	20	21	22	23
24	25	26	27	28	29	30

2023 August

MONDAY
14

TUESDAY
15

WEDNESDAY
16

New Moon

THURSDAY
17

FRIDAY
18

SATURDAY
19

SUNDAY
20

Menus

Grocery

Why are we waiting for someone else to come and fix things? Why aren't we doing it ourselves?

—Malala Yousafzai

To do

August 2023

S	M	T	W	T	F	S
		1	2	3	4	5
6	7	8	9	10	11	12
13	14	15	16	17	18	19
20	21	22	23	24	25	26
27	28	29	30	31		

September 2023

S	M	T	W	T	F	S
					1	2
3	4	5	6	7	8	9
10	11	12	13	14	15	16
17	18	19	20	21	22	23
24	25	26	27	28	29	30

2023 August

MONDAY
21

TUESDAY
22

WEDNESDAY
23

THURSDAY
24

First Quarter Moon

FRIDAY
25

SATURDAY
26

SUNDAY
27

Menus

Grocery

Part of being optimistic is keeping one's head pointed toward the sun, one's feet moving forward.

—Nelson Mandela

To do

August 2023

S	M	T	W	T	F	S
		1	2	3	4	5
6	7	8	9	10	11	12
13	14	15	16	17	18	19
20	21	22	23	24	25	26
27	28	29	30	31		

September 2023

S	M	T	W	T	F	S
					1	2
3	4	5	6	7	8	9
10	11	12	13	14	15	16
17	18	19	20	21	22	23
24	25	26	27	28	29	30

2023 Aug./September

MONDAY *Summer Bank Holiday (UK except SCT)*

28

TUESDAY

29

WEDNESDAY

30

THURSDAY *Full Moon*

31

FRIDAY

1

SATURDAY

2

SUNDAY *Father's Day (AUS, NZ)*

3

Menus

September

SUNDAY	MONDAY	TUESDAY	WEDNESDAY
August 2023 S M T W T F S 1 2 3 4 5 6 7 8 9 10 11 12 13 14 15 16 17 18 19 20 21 22 23 24 25 26 27 28 29 30 31	October 2023 S M T W T F S 1 2 3 4 5 6 7 8 9 10 11 12 13 14 15 16 17 18 19 20 21 22 23 24 25 26 27 28 29 30 31		
3 *Father's Day (AUS, NZ)*	4 *Labor Day (USA, CAN)*	5	6
10	11 *Patriot Day*	12	13
17	18	19	20
24 *Yom Kippur begins*	25	26	27

2023

THURSDAY	FRIDAY	SATURDAY
	1	2
7	8	9
14	15 *Rosh Hashanah begins*	16
21	22	23 *Autumn begins (Northern Hemisphere)*
28	29 *Sukkot begins*	30

Projects

Grocery

Life has been your art. You have set yourself to music. Your days are your sonnets.

—*Oscar Wilde,* The Picture of Dorian Gray

To do

September 2023

S	M	T	W	T	F	S
					1	2
3	4	5	6	7	8	9
10	11	12	13	14	15	16
17	18	19	20	21	22	23
24	25	26	27	28	29	30

October 2023

S	M	T	W	T	F	S
1	2	3	4	5	6	7
8	9	10	11	12	13	14
15	16	17	18	19	20	21
22	23	24	25	26	27	28
29	30	31				

2023 September

MONDAY — *Labor Day (USA, CAN)*
4

TUESDAY
5

WEDNESDAY — *Last Quarter Moon*
6

THURSDAY
7

FRIDAY
8

SATURDAY
9

SUNDAY
10

Menus

Grocery

Great difficulties may be surmounted by patience and perseverance.

—Abigail Adams

To do

September 2023

S	M	T	W	T	F	S
					1	2
3	4	5	6	7	8	9
10	11	12	13	14	15	16
17	18	19	20	21	22	23
24	25	26	27	28	29	30

October 2023

S	M	T	W	T	F	S
1	2	3	4	5	6	7
8	9	10	11	12	13	14
15	16	17	18	19	20	21
22	23	24	25	26	27	28
29	30	31				

2023 September

MONDAY
11
Patriot Day

TUESDAY
12

WEDNESDAY
13

THURSDAY
14

FRIDAY
15
New Moon
Rosh Hashanah begins

SATURDAY
16

SUNDAY
17

Menus

Grocery

We must learn to lift as we climb.

—Angela Davis

To do

September 2023

S	M	T	W	T	F	S
					1	2
3	4	5	6	7	8	9
10	11	12	13	14	15	16
17	18	19	20	21	22	23
24	25	26	27	28	29	30

October 2023

S	M	T	W	T	F	S
1	2	3	4	5	6	7
8	9	10	11	12	13	14
15	16	17	18	19	20	21
22	23	24	25	26	27	28
29	30	31				

2023 September

MONDAY
18

TUESDAY
19

WEDNESDAY
20

THURSDAY
21

FRIDAY
22
First Quarter Moon

SATURDAY
23
Autumn begins (Northern Hemisphere)

SUNDAY
24
Yom Kippur begins

Menus

Grocery

Balance your thoughts with action—if you spend too much time thinking about a thing, you'll never get it done.

—Bruce Lee

To do

September 2023

S	M	T	W	T	F	S
					1	2
3	4	5	6	7	8	9
10	11	12	13	14	15	16
17	18	19	20	21	22	23
24	25	26	27	28	29	30

October 2023

S	M	T	W	T	F	S
1	2	3	4	5	6	7
8	9	10	11	12	13	14
15	16	17	18	19	20	21
22	23	24	25	26	27	28
29	30	31				

2023 Sept./October

MONDAY
25

TUESDAY
26

WEDNESDAY
27

THURSDAY
28

FRIDAY
29

Full Moon
Sukkot begins

SATURDAY
30

SUNDAY
1

Menus

October

SUNDAY	MONDAY	TUESDAY	WEDNESDAY
1	2	3	4
8	9 *Columbus Day (USA); Indigenous Peoples' Day (USA); Thanksgiving Day (CAN)*	10	11
15	16	17	18
22	23	24	25
29	30	31 *Halloween*	

2023

THURSDAY	FRIDAY	SATURDAY
5	6	7
12	13	14
19	20	21
26	27	28

September 2023

S	M	T	W	T	F	S
					1	2
3	4	5	6	7	8	9
10	11	12	13	14	15	16
17	18	19	20	21	22	23
24	25	26	27	28	29	30

November 2023

S	M	T	W	T	F	S
			1	2	3	4
5	6	7	8	9	10	11
12	13	14	15	16	17	18
19	20	21	22	23	24	25
26	27	28	29	30		

Projects

Grocery

I think that's what life is about; it's about learning something new every day.

—Serena Williams

To do

October 2023

S	M	T	W	T	F	S
1	2	3	4	5	6	7
8	9	10	11	12	13	14
15	16	17	18	19	20	21
22	23	24	25	26	27	28
29	30	31				

November 2023

S	M	T	W	T	F	S
			1	2	3	4
5	6	7	8	9	10	11
12	13	14	15	16	17	18
19	20	21	22	23	24	25
26	27	28	29	30		

2023 October

MONDAY
2

TUESDAY
3

WEDNESDAY
4

THURSDAY
5

FRIDAY
6
Last Quarter Moon

SATURDAY
7

SUNDAY
8

Menus

Grocery

When people say there is no alternative, there is always an alternative... You always have this choice.

—Marjane Satrapi

To do

October 2023

S	M	T	W	T	F	S
1	2	3	4	5	6	7
8	9	10	11	12	13	14
15	16	17	18	19	20	21
22	23	24	25	26	27	28
29	30	31				

November 2023

S	M	T	W	T	F	S
			1	2	3	4
5	6	7	8	9	10	11
12	13	14	15	16	17	18
19	20	21	22	23	24	25
26	27	28	29	30		

2023 October

MONDAY
9

Columbus Day (USA)
Indigenous Peoples' Day (USA)
Thanksgiving Day (CAN)

TUESDAY
10

WEDNESDAY
11

THURSDAY
12

FRIDAY
13

SATURDAY
14

New Moon

SUNDAY
15

Menus

Grocery

My only advice is to stay aware, listen carefully, and yell for help if you need it.

—Judy Blume

To do

October 2023

S	M	T	W	T	F	S
1	2	3	4	5	6	7
8	9	10	11	12	13	14
15	16	17	18	19	20	21
22	23	24	25	26	27	28
29	30	31				

November 2023

S	M	T	W	T	F	S
			1	2	3	4
5	6	7	8	9	10	11
12	13	14	15	16	17	18
19	20	21	22	23	24	25
26	27	28	29	30		

2023 October

MONDAY
16

TUESDAY
17

WEDNESDAY
18

THURSDAY
19

FRIDAY
20

SATURDAY
21

SUNDAY
22

First Quarter Moon

Menus

Grocery

A little nonsense now and then is cherished by the wisest men.

—*Roald Dahl,* Charlie and the Great Glass Elevator

To do

October 2023

S	M	T	W	T	F	S
1	2	3	4	5	6	7
8	9	10	11	12	13	14
15	16	17	18	19	20	21
22	23	24	25	26	27	28
29	30	31				

November 2023

S	M	T	W	T	F	S
			1	2	3	4
5	6	7	8	9	10	11
12	13	14	15	16	17	18
19	20	21	22	23	24	25
26	27	28	29	30		

2023 October

MONDAY
23

TUESDAY
24

WEDNESDAY
25

THURSDAY
26

FRIDAY
27

SATURDAY
28

Full Moon

SUNDAY
29

Menus

November

SUNDAY	MONDAY	TUESDAY	WEDNESDAY
October 2023 S M T W T F S 1 2 3 4 5 6 7 8 9 10 11 12 13 14 15 16 17 18 19 20 21 22 23 24 25 26 27 28 29 30 31	December 2023 S M T W T F S 1 2 3 4 5 6 7 8 9 10 11 12 13 14 15 16 17 18 19 20 21 22 23 24/31 25 26 27 28 29 30		1
5 *Daylight Saving Time ends (USA, CAN)*	6	7 *Election Day*	8
12 *Diwali begins*	13	14	15
19	20	21	22
26	27	28	29

2023

THURSDAY	FRIDAY	SATURDAY
2	3	4
9	10	11 *Veterans Day (USA); Remembrance Day (CAN, UK)*
16	17	18
23 *Thanksgiving Day*	24	25
30 *St. Andrew's Day (SCT)*		

Projects

Grocery

We're here for a reason. I believe a bit of the reason is to throw little torches out to lead people through the dark.

—Whoopi Goldberg

To do

November 2023

S	M	T	W	T	F	S
			1	2	3	4
5	6	7	8	9	10	11
12	13	14	15	16	17	18
19	20	21	22	23	24	25
26	27	28	29	30		

December 2023

S	M	T	W	T	F	S
					1	2
3	4	5	6	7	8	9
10	11	12	13	14	15	16
17	18	19	20	21	22	23
24/31	25	26	27	28	29	30

2023 Oct./November

MONDAY
30

TUESDAY
31

Halloween

WEDNESDAY
1

THURSDAY
2

FRIDAY
3

SATURDAY
4

SUNDAY
5

Last Quarter Moon
Daylight Saving Time ends (USA, CAN)

Menus

Grocery

However bad life may seem, there is always something you can do and succeed at. While there's life, there is hope.

—Stephen Hawking

To do

November 2023

S	M	T	W	T	F	S
			1	2	3	4
5	6	7	8	9	10	11
12	13	14	15	16	17	18
19	20	21	22	23	24	25
26	27	28	29	30		

December 2023

S	M	T	W	T	F	S
					1	2
3	4	5	6	7	8	9
10	11	12	13	14	15	16
17	18	19	20	21	22	23
24/31	25	26	27	28	29	30

2023 November

MONDAY
6

TUESDAY
7
Election Day

WEDNESDAY
8

THURSDAY
9

FRIDAY
10

SATURDAY
11
Veterans Day (USA)
Remembrance Day (CAN, UK)

SUNDAY
12
Diwali begins

Menus

Grocery

You're given the form, but you have to write the sonnet yourself. What you say is completely up to you.

—*Madeleine L'Engle,* A Wrinkle in Time

To do

November 2023

S	M	T	W	T	F	S
			1	2	3	4
5	6	7	8	9	10	11
12	13	14	15	16	17	18
19	20	21	22	23	24	25
26	27	28	29	30		

December 2023

S	M	T	W	T	F	S
					1	2
3	4	5	6	7	8	9
10	11	12	13	14	15	16
17	18	19	20	21	22	23
24/31	25	26	27	28	29	30

2023 November

MONDAY
13

New Moon

TUESDAY
14

WEDNESDAY
15

THURSDAY
16

FRIDAY
17

SATURDAY
18

SUNDAY
19

Menus

Grocery

No matter where you are from, your dreams are valid.

—Lupita Nyong'o

To do

November 2023

S	M	T	W	T	F	S
			1	2	3	4
5	6	7	8	9	10	11
12	13	14	15	16	17	18
19	20	21	22	23	24	25
26	27	28	29	30		

December 2023

S	M	T	W	T	F	S
					1	2
3	4	5	6	7	8	9
10	11	12	13	14	15	16
17	18	19	20	21	22	23
24/31	25	26	27	28	29	30

2023 November

MONDAY *First Quarter Moon*

20

TUESDAY

21

WEDNESDAY

22

THURSDAY *Thanksgiving Day*

23

FRIDAY

24

SATURDAY

25

SUNDAY

26

Menus

Grocery

You never really understand a person until you consider things from his point of view...until you climb inside of his skin and walk around in it.

—*Harper Lee,* To Kill a Mockingbird

To do

November 2023

S	M	T	W	T	F	S
			1	2	3	4
5	6	7	8	9	10	11
12	13	14	15	16	17	18
19	20	21	22	23	24	25
26	27	28	29	30		

December 2023

S	M	T	W	T	F	S
					1	2
3	4	5	6	7	8	9
10	11	12	13	14	15	16
17	18	19	20	21	22	23
24/31	25	26	27	28	29	30

2023 Nov./December

MONDAY
27

Full Moon

TUESDAY
28

WEDNESDAY
29

THURSDAY
30

St. Andrew's Day (SCT)

FRIDAY
1

SATURDAY
2

SUNDAY
3

Menus

December

SUNDAY	MONDAY	TUESDAY	WEDNESDAY
November 2023 S M T W T F S 1 2 3 4 5 6 7 8 9 10 11 12 13 14 15 16 17 18 19 20 21 22 23 24 25 26 27 28 29 30	January 2024 S M T W T F S 1 2 3 4 5 6 7 8 9 10 11 12 13 14 15 16 17 18 19 20 21 22 23 24 25 26 27 28 29 30 31		
3	4	5	6
10	11	12	13
17	18	19	20
24 *Christmas Eve* *New Year's Eve* 31	25 *Christmas Day*	26 *Kwanzaa begins; Boxing Day (AUS, CAN, NZ, UK)*	27

2023

THURSDAY	FRIDAY	SATURDAY
	1	2
7 *Hanukkah begins; Pearl Harbor Day*	8	9
14	15	16
21 *Winter begins (Northern Hemisphere)*	22	23
28	29	30

Projects

Grocery

Whatever music you beat on your drum, there is somebody who can dance to it.

—*Chinua Achebe,* Arrow of God

To do

December 2023

S	M	T	W	T	F	S
					1	2
3	4	5	6	7	8	9
10	11	12	13	14	15	16
17	18	19	20	21	22	23
24/31	25	26	27	28	29	30

January 2024

S	M	T	W	T	F	S
	1	2	3	4	5	6
7	8	9	10	11	12	13
14	15	16	17	18	19	20
21	22	23	24	25	26	27
28	29	30	31			

2023 December

MONDAY
4

TUESDAY
5
Last Quarter Moon

WEDNESDAY
6

THURSDAY
7
Hanukkah begins
Pearl Harbor Day

FRIDAY
8

SATURDAY
9

SUNDAY
10

Menus

Grocery

True success is reaching our potential without compromising our values.

—Muhammad Ali

To do

December 2023

S	M	T	W	T	F	S
					1	2
3	4	5	6	7	8	9
10	11	12	13	14	15	16
17	18	19	20	21	22	23
24/31	25	26	27	28	29	30

January 2024

S	M	T	W	T	F	S
	1	2	3	4	5	6
7	8	9	10	11	12	13
14	15	16	17	18	19	20
21	22	23	24	25	26	27
28	29	30	31			

2023 December

MONDAY
11

TUESDAY
12

New Moon

WEDNESDAY
13

THURSDAY
14

FRIDAY
15

SATURDAY
16

SUNDAY
17

Menus

Grocery

Do whatever brings you to life, then. Follow your own fascinations, obsessions, and compulsions. Trust them. Create whatever causes a revolution in your heart.

—Elizabeth Gilbert

To do

December 2023

S	M	T	W	T	F	S
					1	2
3	4	5	6	7	8	9
10	11	12	13	14	15	16
17	18	19	20	21	22	23
24/31	25	26	27	28	29	30

January 2024

S	M	T	W	T	F	S
	1	2	3	4	5	6
7	8	9	10	11	12	13
14	15	16	17	18	19	20
21	22	23	24	25	26	27
28	29	30	31			

2023 December

MONDAY
18

TUESDAY
19
First Quarter Moon

WEDNESDAY
20

THURSDAY
21
Winter begins (Northern Hemisphere)

FRIDAY
22

SATURDAY
23

SUNDAY
24
Christmas Eve

Menus

Grocery

Nurture your mind with great thoughts. To believe in the heroic makes heroes.

—Benjamin Disraeli

To do

December 2023

S	M	T	W	T	F	S
					1	2
3	4	5	6	7	8	9
10	11	12	13	14	15	16
17	18	19	20	21	22	23
24/31	25	26	27	28	29	30

January 2024

S	M	T	W	T	F	S
	1	2	3	4	5	6
7	8	9	10	11	12	13
14	15	16	17	18	19	20
21	22	23	24	25	26	27
28	29	30	31			

2023 December

MONDAY *Christmas Day*
25

TUESDAY *Kwanzaa begins*
Boxing Day (AUS, CAN, NZ, UK)
26

WEDNESDAY *Full Moon*
27

THURSDAY
28

FRIDAY
29

SATURDAY
30

SUNDAY *New Year's Eve*
31

Menus

2024 Planning Calendar

JANUARY

S	M	T	W	T	F	S
	1	2	3	4	5	6
7	8	9	10	11	12	13
14	15	16	17	18	19	20
21	22	23	24	25	26	27
28	29	30	31			

FEBRUARY

S	M	T	W	T	F	S
				1	2	3
4	5	6	7	8	9	10
11	12	13	14	15	16	17
18	19	20	21	22	23	24
25	26	27	28	29		

MARCH

S	M	T	W	T	F	S
					1	2
3	4	5	6	7	8	9
10	11	12	13	14	15	16
17	18	19	20	21	22	23
24	25	26	27	28	29	30
31						

APRIL

S	M	T	W	T	F	S
	1	2	3	4	5	6
7	8	9	10	11	12	13
14	15	16	17	18	19	20
21	22	23	24	25	26	27
28	29	30				

MAY

S	M	T	W	T	F	S
			1	2	3	4
5	6	7	8	9	10	11
12	13	14	15	16	17	18
19	20	21	22	23	24	25
26	27	28	29	30	31	

JUNE

S	M	T	W	T	F	S
						1
2	3	4	5	6	7	8
9	10	11	12	13	14	15
16	17	18	19	20	21	22
23	24	25	26	27	28	29
30						

2024 Planning Calendar

JULY

S	M	T	W	T	F	S
	1	2	3	4	5	6
7	8	9	10	11	12	13
14	15	16	17	18	19	20
21	22	23	24	25	26	27
28	29	30	31			

AUGUST

S	M	T	W	T	F	S
				1	2	3
4	5	6	7	8	9	10
11	12	13	14	15	16	17
18	19	20	21	22	23	24
25	26	27	28	29	30	31

SEPTEMBER

S	M	T	W	T	F	S
1	2	3	4	5	6	7
8	9	10	11	12	13	14
15	16	17	18	19	20	21
22	23	24	25	26	27	28
29	30					

OCTOBER

S	M	T	W	T	F	S
		1	2	3	4	5
6	7	8	9	10	11	12
13	14	15	16	17	18	19
20	21	22	23	24	25	26
27	28	29	30	31		

NOVEMBER

S	M	T	W	T	F	S
					1	2
3	4	5	6	7	8	9
10	11	12	13	14	15	16
17	18	19	20	21	22	23
24	25	26	27	28	29	30

DECEMBER

S	M	T	W	T	F	S
1	2	3	4	5	6	7
8	9	10	11	12	13	14
15	16	17	18	19	20	21
22	23	24	25	26	27	28
29	30	31				

Babysitters' Information

You are at:

Name: ____________________

Address: ____________________

City: ____________________ State: __________ Zip: __________

The phone number here is: ____________________

In case of an emergency, call 911

and: ____________________

Poison Control: ____________________

Our cell # is: ____________________

We will be at:

Place self-stick notepad here.

Meal/snack instructions:

Let Us Introduce Our Children

Name: ______

Age: ______ Bedtime: ______

Likes/Dislikes: ______

Favorite Things: ______

Allergies/Medical: ______

Name: ______

Age: ______ Bedtime: ______

Likes/Dislikes: ______

Favorite Things: ______

Allergies/Medical: ______

Name: ______

Age: ______ Bedtime: ______

Likes/Dislikes: ______

Favorite Things: ______

Allergies/Medical: ______

Name: ______

Age: ______ Bedtime: ______

Likes/Dislikes: ______

Favorite Things: ______

Allergies/Medical: ______

Babysitters' Phone Numbers

Name:	Phone Number:

Children's Friends

Name:	Parent:	Phone Number:

Quick Reference Children's Organizations

Child's Name: ________________
Organization/Team: ________________

Leader: ________________
Phone: ________________
Meeting/Practice:
M__ T__ W__ TH__ F__ S__ SU__
Carpool: ________________
Snacks/Refreshments: ________________

Child's Name: ________________
Organization/Team: ________________

Leader: ________________
Phone: ________________
Meeting/Practice:
M__ T__ W__ TH__ F__ S__ SU__
Carpool: ________________
Snacks/Refreshments: ________________

Child's Name: ________________
Organization/Team: ________________

Leader: ________________
Phone: ________________
Meeting/Practice:
M__ T__ W__ TH__ F__ S__ SU__
Carpool: ________________
Snacks/Refreshments: ________________

Child's Name: ________________
Organization/Team: ________________

Leader: ________________
Phone: ________________
Meeting/Practice:
M__ T__ W__ TH__ F__ S__ SU__
Carpool: ________________
Snacks/Refreshments: ________________

Child's Name: ________________
Organization/Team: ________________

Leader: ________________
Phone: ________________
Meeting/Practice:
M__ T__ W__ TH__ F__ S__ SU__
Carpool: ________________
Snacks/Refreshments: ________________

Child's Name: ________________
Organization/Team: ________________

Leader: ________________
Phone: ________________
Meeting/Practice:
M__ T__ W__ TH__ F__ S__ SU__
Carpool: ________________
Snacks/Refreshments: ________________

Quick Reference Children's Organizations

Child's Name: ____________________
Organization/Team: ____________________
____
Leader: ____________________
Phone: ____________________
Meeting/Practice:
M__ T__ W__ TH__ F__ S__ SU__
Carpool: ____________________
Snacks/Refreshments: ____________________
____
____

Child's Name: ____________________
Organization/Team: ____________________
____
Leader: ____________________
Phone: ____________________
Meeting/Practice:
M__ T__ W__ TH__ F__ S__ SU__
Carpool: ____________________
Snacks/Refreshments: ____________________
____
____

Child's Name: ____________________
Organization/Team: ____________________
____
Leader: ____________________
Phone: ____________________
Meeting/Practice:
M__ T__ W__ TH__ F__ S__ SU__
Carpool: ____________________
Snacks/Refreshments: ____________________
____
____

Child's Name: ____________________
Organization/Team: ____________________
____
Leader: ____________________
Phone: ____________________
Meeting/Practice:
M__ T__ W__ TH__ F__ S__ SU__
Carpool: ____________________
Snacks/Refreshments: ____________________
____
____

Child's Name: ____________________
Organization/Team: ____________________
____
Leader: ____________________
Phone: ____________________
Meeting/Practice:
M__ T__ W__ TH__ F__ S__ SU__
Carpool: ____________________
Snacks/Refreshments: ____________________
____
____

Child's Name: ____________________
Organization/Team: ____________________
____
Leader: ____________________
Phone: ____________________
Meeting/Practice:
M__ T__ W__ TH__ F__ S__ SU__
Carpool: ____________________
Snacks/Refreshments: ____________________
____
____

Quick Reference Parents' Organizations

Organization/Team: ______________________

____

Leader: ______________________

Phone: ______________________

Meeting/Practice:

M__ T__ W__ TH__ F__ S__ SU__

Carpool: ______________________

Snacks/Refreshments: ______________________

____

____

____

Organization/Team: ______________________

____

Leader: ______________________

Phone: ______________________

Meeting/Practice:

M__ T__ W__ TH__ F__ S__ SU__

Carpool: ______________________

Snacks/Refreshments: ______________________

____

____

____

Organization/Team: ______________________

____

Leader: ______________________

Phone: ______________________

Meeting/Practice:

M__ T__ W__ TH__ F__ S__ SU__

Carpool: ______________________

Snacks/Refreshments: ______________________

____

____

____

Organization/Team: ______________________

____

Leader: ______________________

Phone: ______________________

Meeting/Practice:

M__ T__ W__ TH__ F__ S__ SU__

Carpool: ______________________

Snacks/Refreshments: ______________________

____

____

____

Organization/Team: ______________________

____

Leader: ______________________

Phone: ______________________

Meeting/Practice:

M__ T__ W__ TH__ F__ S__ SU__

Carpool: ______________________

Snacks/Refreshments: ______________________

____

____

____

Organization/Team: ______________________

____

Leader: ______________________

Phone: ______________________

Meeting/Practice:

M__ T__ W__ TH__ F__ S__ SU__

Carpool: ______________________

Snacks/Refreshments: ______________________

____

____

____

Quick Reference Address/Phone

Name: ______________________

Address: ______________________

City: ______________________

State/Zip: ______________________

Home Phone: ______________________

Work Phone: ______________________

Fax: __________ Cell: __________

Email: ______________________

Name: ______________________

Address: ______________________

City: ______________________

State/Zip: ______________________

Home Phone: ______________________

Work Phone: ______________________

Fax: __________ Cell: __________

Email: ______________________

Name: ______________________

Address: ______________________

City: ______________________

State/Zip: ______________________

Home Phone: ______________________

Work Phone: ______________________

Fax: __________ Cell: __________

Email: ______________________

Name: ______________________

Address: ______________________

City: ______________________

State/Zip: ______________________

Home Phone: ______________________

Work Phone: ______________________

Fax: __________ Cell: __________

Email: ______________________

Name: ______________________

Address: ______________________

City: ______________________

State/Zip: ______________________

Home Phone: ______________________

Work Phone: ______________________

Fax: __________ Cell: __________

Email: ______________________

Name: ______________________

Address: ______________________

City: ______________________

State/Zip: ______________________

Home Phone: ______________________

Work Phone: ______________________

Fax: __________ Cell: __________

Email: ______________________

Quick Reference Address/Phone

Name: ____________________
Address: ____________________
City: ____________________
State/Zip: ____________________
Home Phone: ____________________
Work Phone: ____________________
Fax: __________ Cell: __________
Email: ____________________

Name: ____________________
Address: ____________________
City: ____________________
State/Zip: ____________________
Home Phone: ____________________
Work Phone: ____________________
Fax: __________ Cell: __________
Email: ____________________

Name: ____________________
Address: ____________________
City: ____________________
State/Zip: ____________________
Home Phone: ____________________
Work Phone: ____________________
Fax: __________ Cell: __________
Email: ____________________

Name: ____________________
Address: ____________________
City: ____________________
State/Zip: ____________________
Home Phone: ____________________
Work Phone: ____________________
Fax: __________ Cell: __________
Email: ____________________

Name: ____________________
Address: ____________________
City: ____________________
State/Zip: ____________________
Home Phone: ____________________
Work Phone: ____________________
Fax: __________ Cell: __________
Email: ____________________

Name: ____________________
Address: ____________________
City: ____________________
State/Zip: ____________________
Home Phone: ____________________
Work Phone: ____________________
Fax: __________ Cell: __________
Email: ____________________

Additional Phone Numbers

Church: ______________________

Hair Salon: ______________________

Library: ______________________

Attorney: ______________________

Accountant: ______________________

Bank: ______________________

Bank: ______________________

Insurance Agency: ______________________

Post Office: ______________________

Veterinarian: ______________________

Favorite Restaurants:

____

____

____

Travel Agent: ______________________

Florist: ______________________

Other Numbers:

Name: Number:

____

____

____

____

____

____

____

Notes

Notes

Notes

Notes

Notes

Notes

Happy Birthday!	Happy Birthday!	Happy Birthday!	Happy Birthday!	Happy Birthday!	Happy Birthday!	Happy Birthday!	Happy Birthday!	Happy Birthday!
Happy Birthday!	Happy Birthday!	Happy Birthday!	Happy Birthday!	Happy Birthday!	Happy Birthday!	Happy Birthday!	Happy Birthday!	Happy Birthday!
Party!	Party!	Party!	Party!	Party!	Party!	Party!	Party!	Party!
Meeting!	Meeting!	Meeting!	Meeting!	Meeting!	Meeting!	Meeting!	Meeting!	Meeting!
Meeting!	Meeting!	Meeting!	Meeting!	Meeting!	Meeting!	Meeting!	Meeting!	Meeting!
Travel	Travel	Travel	Travel	Travel	Travel	Travel	Travel	Travel
Travel	Travel	Travel	Travel	Travel	Travel	Travel	Travel	Travel
Dentist	Dentist	Dentist	Dentist	Dentist	Dentist	Dentist	Dentist	Dentist
Doctor	Doctor	Doctor	Doctor	Doctor	Doctor	Doctor	Doctor	Doctor
Girls Night	Girls Night	Girls Night	Girls Night	Girls Night	Vet	Vet	Vet	Vet
Date Night	Date Night	Date Night	Date Night	Date Night	Date Night	Date Night	Date Night	Date Night
Family Vacation	Family Vacation	Family Vacation	Family Vacation	Family Vacation	Family Vacation	Family Vacation	Family Vacation	Family Vacation
Important	Important	Important	Important	Important	Important	Important	Important	Important

School Event	School Event	School Event	School Event	School Event	School Event	School Event	School Event	School Event
No School	No School	No School	No School	No School	No School	No School	No School	No School
No School	No School	No School	No School	No School	No School	No School	No School	No School
1/2 School Day	1/2 School Day	1/2 School Day	1/2 School Day	1/2 School Day	1/2 School Day	1/2 School Day	1/2 School Day	1/2 School Day
Concert	Concert	Concert	Concert	Concert	Rehearsal	Rehearsal	Rehearsal	Rehearsal
Game	Game	Game	Game	Game	Game	Game	Game	Game
Game	Game	Game	Game	Game	Game	Game	Game	Game
Practice	Practice	Practice	Practice	Practice	Practice	Practice	Practice	Practice
Practice	Practice	Practice	Practice	Practice	Practice	Practice	Practice	Practice
Volunteer	Volunteer	Volunteer	Volunteer	Volunteer	Volunteer	Volunteer	Volunteer	Volunteer
Repair	Repair	Repair	Repair	Repair	Repair	Repair	Repair	Repair
Pay Day	Pay Day	Pay Day	Pay Day	Pay Day	Pay Day	Pay Day	Pay Day	Pay Day
Pay Day	Pay Day	Pay Day	Pay Day	Pay Day	Pay Day	Pay Day	Pay Day	Pay Day

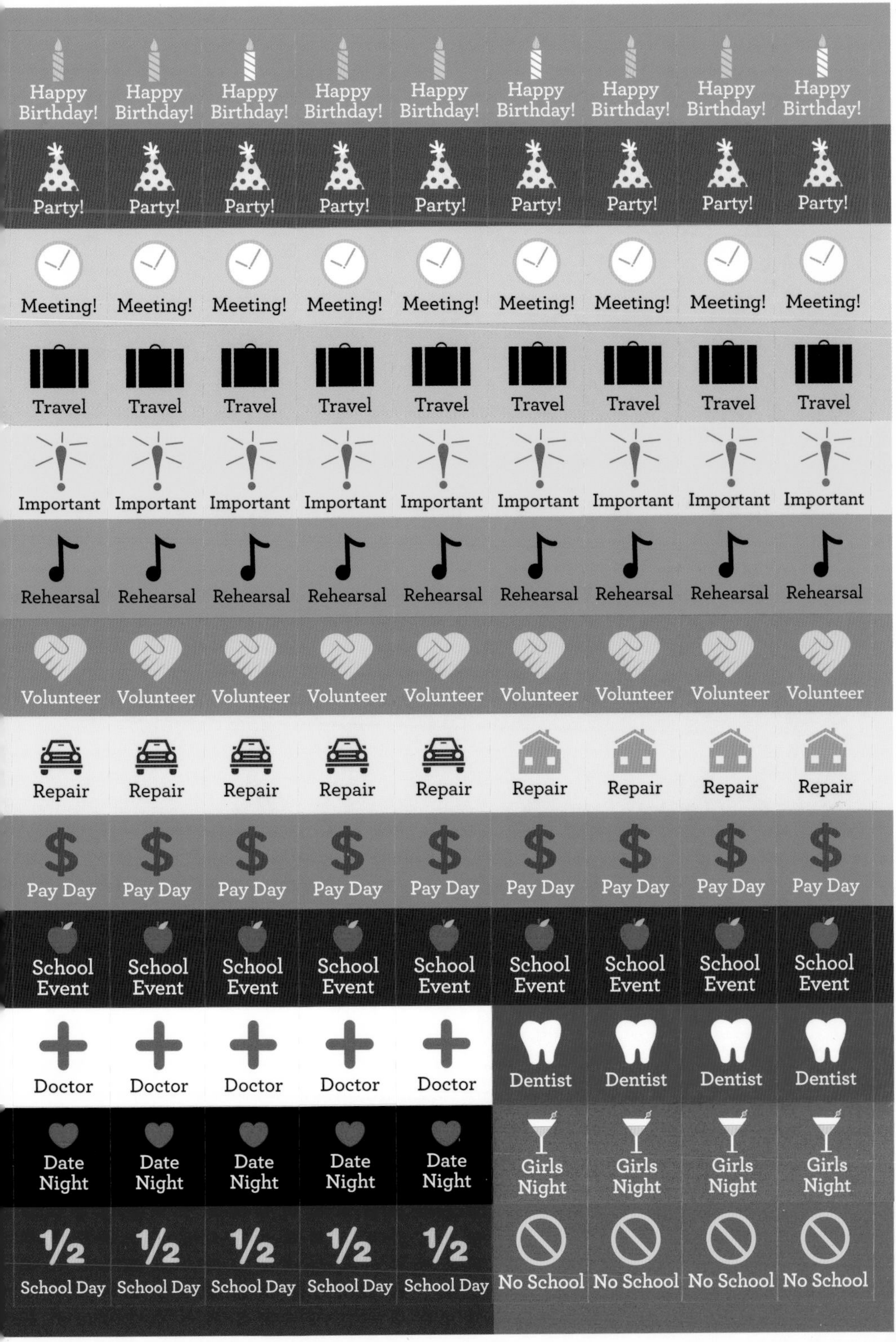
Happy Birthday! Happy Birthday! Happy Birthday! Happy Birthday! Happy Birthday! Happy Birthday! Happy Birthday! Happy Birthday! Happy Birthday!
Party! Party! Party! Party! Party! Party! Party! Party! Party!
Meeting! Meeting! Meeting! Meeting! Meeting! Meeting! Meeting! Meeting! Meeting!
Travel Travel Travel Travel Travel Travel Travel Travel Travel
Important Important Important Important Important Important Important Important Important
Rehearsal Rehearsal Rehearsal Rehearsal Rehearsal Rehearsal Rehearsal Rehearsal Rehearsal
Volunteer Volunteer Volunteer Volunteer Volunteer Volunteer Volunteer Volunteer Volunteer
Repair Repair Repair Repair Repair Repair Repair Repair Repair
Pay Day Pay Day Pay Day Pay Day Pay Day Pay Day Pay Day Pay Day Pay Day
School Event School Event School Event School Event School Event School Event School Event School Event School Event
Doctor Doctor Doctor Doctor Doctor Dentist Dentist Dentist Dentist
Date Night Date Night Date Night Date Night Date Night Girls Night Girls Night Girls Night Girls Night
1/2 School Day 1/2 School Day 1/2 School Day 1/2 School Day 1/2 School Day No School No School No School No School